THE ULTIMATE FIRST TIME TRAVELLER'S GUIDE TO ITALY

Ambreen Hameed

Table of Contents

Introduction

Italy is a country that attracts many tourists, with its famous landmarks of Rome, the romantic vibe of Venice, and the art and architecture of Florence. This is also where you can find the breathtaking Lake Como, the Leaning Tower of Pisa, and of course, the Vatican City.

In many people's eyes, Italy is a magical and romantic country. People fall in love with the place and return time and again. Some even decide to move there! The country's art, architecture, history, and sceneries are indeed stunning.

It is an island country in the Mediterranean Sea, surrounded by France, Switzerland, Austria, and Monaco. It's famous for its food, fashion, landscapes, and culture. There are so many things to see here; the good thing is that it's pretty easy to visit from any part of the world.

When you visit Italy, there is so much to see and do that it will be impossible to tick off everything on your bucket list in one trip. The best advice is to create a shortlist of things you want to see and visit each place on the list as time allows. Getting around Italy is easy—you can hire a car and drive or take a train or plane.

This travel guide will give you all the information you need to have a great time in Italy. We'll cover fun facts, language, culture, and their mouth-watering food. Want to shop 'til you drop? Our tips on where to go will help you out! Want to see art like nowhere else in the world? Or perhaps you want to go on a nature trip? The list goes on!

So without further ado, let's get started!

Chapter 1
The Most Beautiful Boot in the World - Italy!

If you've ever looked at a map of Italy, you will notice that its shape is like a boot. The toe of Italy is actually the famous Sicily!

Italy's unique shape is just one of the amazing facts about this country. Only a few countries have the same allure as Italy, and whether it is food, art, music, theatre, sport, beauty, nature, fashion, or history, Italy will surely tick every box on your checklist.

Italy is relatively small compared to some other countries, it is just 301,338 square kilometers, but it certainly is packed with many beautiful tourist spots. With a population of 60 million (in 2018), the country has a strong tourism industry, and during the summer months, the number of people visiting the country increases. So you can expect a lot of queues between July and August in particular, but this country is busy year-round.

Most people would picture Rome when they hear 'Italy,' but what about Milan, Florence, Venice, Pisa, Pompeii, Lake Garda, Lake Como, Naples, Turin, and Verona? Definitely, this is a country that has more famous cities than any other in the world. So, with that in mind, let us learn more about this fascinating country.

Quick & Interesting Facts You Need to Know

Capital - Rome

Dialing Code - + 39

Population - 60.42 million (in 2018)

Currency - Euro

Language - Italian

Time Zone - Central European Standard Time (GMT + 1)

Religion - Christianity, Catholic

Bordering Countries - France, Switzerland, Slovenia, Australia

- Europe has three active volcanoes, and they're all found in Italy, namely Etna, Stromboli, and Vesuvius
- Rome (the capital) was founded way back in 753BC

- Italy's highest peak is Mont Blanc, standing at a vast 4807m in the Alps
- The Italian flag consists of three colors, which all represent a theme - green (hope), white (faith), and red (charity)
- The ancient Roman Empire left behind many fantastic buildings and sites of architecture but ended in 395AD
- Italy is the world's fifth most visited country
- Italy is Europe's most prominent earthquake spot, although they are pretty rare still
- Vatican City (in Rome itself) is classified as a country, and it is the smallest country on earth
- The concept of a basilica was born in Italy and then evolved to mean a Catholic pilgrimage site
- Italy is home to many castles, such as the Ussel Castle, the Verrès Castle, and the Valle d'Aosta Fort Bard.
- The University of Bologna is the oldest in the world, dating back to 1088
- Italy is home to many internationally renowned fashion houses, including Armani, Prada, Gucci, Versace, and Benetton. Italians take clothing very seriously.
- Our favorite "Pasta" dates back to the 4th century BC!
- Naples is the home of pizza, and it was invented in 1860

- Italy introduced the use of the fork to the world, thanks to their love of eating pasta!
- Many hotels in Italy don't have a 17th floor because the number is considered unlucky and has associations with death
- Never place a hat on a bed in Italy because it is regarded as bad luck
- Black cats are known to bring misfortune in Italy
- There is a belief in Italy that if someone brushes over the feet with a broom, that person is never going to get married
- You cannot visit Poveglia Island in Italy because it is considered a far too haunted place!
- Get your hiking shoes ready because 4/5 of the country consists of hills or mountains
- You will find more artistic masterpieces in Italy per square mile than anywhere else in the world
- Never sit on the steps of a church or in a church courtyard while eating or drinking, else you will get penalized
- Italians always stand up when an elderly walks into the room as a sign of respect

In Italy, family is very important. The Italians believe that the family is the center of society and are very proud of their heritage. Therefore, they spend many hours together as a family, going on trips and eating together on special occasions. In addition, many Italians believe in religion and pridefully practice Catholic traditions.

Ciao Bella! Quick Italian Phrases to Learn

Italy is a country where English is very common, especially in the major cities where many tourists visit every single day of the year. However, despite that, you must admit that Italian is such a beautiful language that deserves learning.

Language is a big part of Italian culture. Therefore, locals will certainly appreciate it if you say some phrases in their native tongue; in return, they will be warm and welcoming to you.

Here are the common Italian phrases and words that will be most useful to you on your travels:

- Hello / Hi – Ciao
- Goodbye - Addio or Arrivederci
- Please - Per favore
- Yes - Si
- No – No
- Cheers! – Salute!
- Thank you - Grazie
- You're welcome - Prego
- Excuse me (to pass by) - Permesso
- Excuse me (for attention) - Mi scusi
- I'm sorry - Mi dispiace
- I don't understand – Non-capisco

- I don't speak Italian – Non-parlo Italiano
- Do you speak English? - Parla Inglese?
- Can you help me? - Puoi aiutarmi?
- Where is... ? – Dov'è...?
- Entrance – Entrata
- Exit – Uscita –
- Left – Sinistra
- Right – Destra
- Straight ahead – Dritto
- Forward – Avanti
- Back – Dietro
- How are you? - Come stai?
- Good morning - Buon giorno
- Good afternoon - Buona sera
- Good night - Buona note
- My name is - Mi chiamo
- What is your name? - Come si chiama?
- Pleased to meet you – Piacere
- Good thank you - Bene grazie
- At what time? - A che ora?
- In the morning - Di Mattina
- In the afternoon - Di pomeriggio
- In the evening - Di Sera
- Noon – Mezzogiorno
- Can I see the menu, please? - Il menu, per favore?
- What do you recommend? - Che cosa ci consiglia?
- Appetizer – Antipasto –

- First course – Primo
- Second course – Secondo
- Dessert – Dolci
- Red/white wine – Vino rosso/bianco
- House wine – Vino della casa
- The check (bill) please – Il conto, per favore
- Can I pay by card? – Posso pagare con la carta?
- Where's the restroom? – Dov'è il bagno?
- When does it open/close? – Quando si apri / chiude?
- Two adults/one child – Due adulti / un bambino
- One/two ticket/s – Un / due biglietto/i
- Where is the bag store/cloak room?
- Where is the train station? – Dov'è la stazione?
- Where is the bus stop? – Dov'è la fermata
- Newstand (for bus tickets) – Tabacchi

The Italian language is soft and almost sounds like you're singing when you speak. Give it a try; you'll probably fall in love with their language too!

The Dos and Don'ts of Visiting Italy

Every country has its cultural quirks and eccentricities, and it's worth knowing these so as not to accidentally insult a local!

The good news is that Italy's tourism industry is so huge that locals are used to people from all over the world visiting their country. Italian people are warm, welcoming, and kind and will happily help you if needed. In addition, they're also very understanding.

Despite that fact, traveling responsibly means being aware of their culture too. So, here are some of the few things that you should remember when visiting Italy:

Dos

- Do plan your time - If you fail to do this, you will likely miss out on so many amazing sights and experiences! Of course, you don't have to walk around with an itinerary and a clipboard, but a general idea of where you will go every morning will certainly help!
- Do keep your bag close to you at all times - Pickpockets are widespread in large cities, especially in Rome

- Do try to dress well. Italians are very fashionable people, so it will be a good idea to always come out at your best!
- Do look in both directions before you cross a road - Italian driving is often described as 'crazy' at best!
- Do carry some cash with you at all times, as not all shops and restaurants accept cards
- Do remember to look after your belongings
- Do start your morning with a cappuccino and end your evening with an espresso
- Do ask for ice if you want it because it won't come automatically

Don'ts

- Don't wear inappropriate clothing when visiting any church or cathedral. It won't be a good idea to wear shorts, show your shoulders, or wear short skirts when visiting these places. Most churches don't allow people to go inside if they are not properly dressed. This is simply about showing respect to the sacred place
- Don't put your hand/s on someone's lap during a meal
- Don't stretch your arms while at the table.
- Don't leave the table until everyone has finished eating.

- Don't say "ciao" to someone you just met. It is reserved for greeting friends and acquaintances.
- Don't get upset if locals cut in line - queuing isn't as strict in Italy!
- Don't try and use your hands to talk (like the locals), as there are specific hand gestures you don't want to use!
- Don't wear flip-flops in large cities unless you want aching feet at the end of the day!
- Don't forget to try and say a few words of the language, and you can get an extra brownie for it!

By now, you should start to feel excited about your up-and-coming visit to this stunning country. So, when do you plan to go? Let's talk about the weather and good timing next.

Chapter 2
Italy's Climate and When to Visit

Italy is a year-round tourist destination, but summer is undoubtedly the busiest time in most cities and resorts. In addition, of course, Italy enjoys a Mediterranean climate, which means they have long and hot summers, with very little rain and mild but wet winters.

Moreover, Italy is a hilly and mountainous country with coastlines that stretch along the Mediterranean Sea. Therefore, depending on where you want to go, you can expect a few differences in the weather.

Climate Information You Need to Know

It will be about the shoulder seasons for you if you are keen to have more sightseeing, as most people are. The height of summer falls between July and the end of August, and during these times, you will experience crowded streets, heat, and somewhat stressful experiences if you're trying to see the main sights, especially in Rome! However, this is a great time to hit the beaches and enjoy the blue waters.

April to the end of June and September to October are the best times to explore Italy. During these months, temperatures will be warm, and you can still get your skin tanned without the extreme heat like in the peak summer months. April and October may bring a higher chance of rain. Even if there are showers, it won't be a heavy downpour that can ruin your time! These months are also lower in cost compared to the peak summer months. This applies not only to accommodation but airplane ticket prices as well. So, if you want a good deal, check out the spring and autumn months.

The country's north tends to be a little cooler than the south, which is quite typical of the Mediterranean climate. In addition, if you head towards the mountains, you will find cooler weather and a higher chance of rain. During the winter months, e.g., November to February, you can also experience snow. Remember, Italy has several ski resorts, specifically in the Alps, so you'd better prepare for a winter adventure!

During the summer months, between July and August, it's not unusual for temperatures to hit 30 degrees, especially during a heatwave. Locals and tourists flock to the coastal resorts at this time to enjoy the beach and benefit from the sea breeze, which is always inviting.

Important Public Holidays and Celebrations

Italy has several significant public holidays and celebrations you must be aware of before planning your visit. This is for two main reasons. Firstly, you can expect more crowds during large festivals, so you can avoid them if you are looking for some quiet time in the country. Secondly, you may want to plan your vacation for a specific time if you intend to be a part of the festivities!

Here are a few of the most notable holidays and celebrations in Italy that you should be aware of:

1 January - New Year's Day

Like the rest of the world, Italy loves a New Year's party, and with so many festivities the night before, people have the day off on the first day of the year. You will also find that most businesses and shops are closed on this day, but the main city squares are full of families heading out to visit their other relatives. Street entertainment in large cities is also common during this time. If you want to be traditional, head to a lido (a large public swimming pool or beach area) in the morning and enjoy a chilly swim on the first of the year. It's a tradition that will require a hot coffee to warm you up afterward!

6 January - Epiphany

This is the official end of the Christmas period. If you're lucky enough to be around the Vatican at this time, you will see many festivities and a large procession of people dressed in costumes dating back to medieval times who are carrying gifts to the Pope. There is also a large mass at Saint Peter's Basilica.

Easter (date varies but March or April)

Easter Sunday is a big celebration in Italy. There are several masses in all churches, especially in Vatican City. You will also see many chocolate eggs, especially if you are in Florence and close to the famous Duomo. Throughout the week leading up to Easter Sunday (Holy Week), you'll also find many different events and children painting eggs to be hidden for the egg hunt on a Sunday. On Easter Monday, shops and businesses are closed, and most locals will head to beaches or the hills for picnics and days in the sun. The weather at this time is warming up, so it's a great time to get outside. You will also find musical concerts and events up and down the country.

25 April - Liberation Day & St Mark's Day

Liberation Day is a special memorial day in Italy, which marks the end of World War 2. You'll find celebrations up and down the country and concerts, markets, and gastronomical delights to try. If you're in Venice, this is also St Mark's Day, and you'll find great fun in St Mark's Square.

1 May - Labor Day

Labor Day celebrates the hard-working individuals in Italy and grants everyone the day off. You will see different events and parades all over the country and find that the main cities and tourist attractions are bustling at this time. If you want to avoid crowds, perhaps try and avoid visiting between Liberation Day and Labor Day!

2 June - Republic Day

This is a special day in Italy, which marks the start of the Republic itself. In case you're not yet aware, the country's official name is the Republic of Italy! Again, there will be parades and events, and Rome is the main attraction for fun and festivities, especially if you head to the Quirinale, where there is a big military concert.

15 August - Assumption Day

The 'Ferragosto' is a big thing in Italy. This is when the main summer holidays begin for locals, so again you will find huge crowds. On this day, you will also find that many businesses are closed, and most locals head off to the beach and enjoy the sun. You might even find fireworks and parades to mark the big day.

1 November - All Saints Day

This is a day that marks all saints, followed by All Souls Day, when families head to gravesites to leave flowers for deceased family members.

24 and 25 December – Christmas Eve and Day

As with most countries in the region, Christmas is a huge celebration and is spent with family. Italy is all about family, and at this time of year, relatives travel from far and wide to be with their loved ones. You will see nativity plays performed by children in their schools in the days leading up to Christmas and with big family feasts in most homes. On Christmas Day itself, everything will be closed. If you want to visit a Christmas market, the best time is during the week leading up to Christmas, as there will be a festive vibe in the air!

25 December - St Stephen's Day

This public holiday is dedicated to St Stephen (or Stanton Stefano). Again, many places will be closed, but not as many as on Christmas Day itself.

Since Italy is a very popular country to visit, you will see many concerts and other stage performances throughout the year, especially during summer. Therefore, it's a good idea to check online before you visit to see the upcoming shows or events on your chosen dates.

When is The Best Time to Visit Italy?

Most people want to avoid crowds and extremely hot weather conditions. In that case, April to June (Spring) and the end of September into late October (Fall) are the best times. This is because you can find lower prices at this time and experience lower temperatures. On the other hand, the peak summer months (July to August) aren't just hot and crowded. Still, they are certainly more expensive too, as the accommodation prices, airfare, and other travel arrangements like tours are incredibly high.

Of course, Italy should be on top of your list if you are looking for a winter holiday destination. In most resorts, the ski season begins in late November and runs into the middle of April. The most popular time (and therefore the most expensive) is December to February. If you want to head off on a city break, remember that the winter months (anytime between November and the end of March) will be cold and a little wet in most locations. However, there are also many warm and sunny days in-between. The further north you go, the more likely this scenario is. But, the further south you go, the more chance you have of pleasant, Mediterranean weather - it's not surprising to be sitting on the beach in the sunshine during February (with a jacket, of course!).

Italy should be on top of your list if you're looking for a winter holiday destination. The ski season begins in late November and lasts until April in most resorts. Although the most popular time (and therefore the most expensive) is December to February, the weather is cold and a little wet in most areas. Then again, there are also many warm and sunny days in-between. So, naturally, the further north you go, the more likely this scenario is. But, if you are travelling south, the more chance you'll have pleasant Mediterranean weather—it's not surprising to sit on the beach in February.

Chapter 3
Getting To and Around Italy

Italy is a European country that shares land borders with other countries. There are several ways you can get there: You can fly directly, indirectly or by train or bus. It's a great idea to find out which option is best for you.

During the lean months, you can get some very cheap fares from other European cities, with low-cost airlines flying to Rome and Milan in particular.

Let's check out each option in detail!

Flying to Italy

Italian cities are served by many big airlines, with planes flying direct daily. There are several major airports across the country, but the main ones are:

- Rome - Fiumicino and Ciampino. The first option is the larger of the two, with Ciampino being aimed towards low cost and budget flights
- Milan - Malpensa and Linate

- Bologna - Guglielmo Marconi
- Naples - Capodichino
- Pisa - Galileo Galilei
- Vince - Marco Polo and Treviso
- Turin - Sandro Pertini
- Palermo - Punta Raisi
- Catania - Vincenzo Bellini
- Bari - Palese
- Genoa - Cristoforo Colombo

Rome, Milan, and Venice airports are the busiest in Italy, and during the summer months, in particular, you will see numerous daily flights.

All airports have road links to the city center, which makes it easy to get from the airport to the city center. In addition, most have shuttle buses for a small cost, and many taxis are available outside the terminal. However, before getting in a cab, you should negotiate with the driver on the price first. Otherwise, they will ask you to pay a higher amount.

Travel by Train

Another option is to travel from another European country via train. There's an extensive network of trains connecting major cities, and if you buy a rail pass, you can use it on a set number of journeys within the allowed pass duration. This is called "inter-railing," You can choose from several countries to include in your trip (with Italy having one of the most famous rails passes available), or go for a continent-wide pass and explore on your own schedule. If you want to see changing landscapes and dramatic countryside views while saving money, inter-railing is the best way to travel!

Train routes and fares change on a regular basis and also depend upon the season you're travelling. Therefore, it's a good idea to check online before you head off, but the main routes that you should take note of are the following:

- From Austria, travelling via Vienna
- From France, stopping at Paris, Nice, and Lyon
- From Germany, travelling via Munich
- From Spain, travelling via Barcelona
- From Switzerland, travelling via Zurich, Basel, and Geneva

Rail passes exist for all these routes and can be purchased either at main railway stations or online. Check all your options to find the best deal, as some of these can save you Euros, which can be put to great use once you arrive.

Buses and Self-Driving

Buses and self-drive are options you might like to consider when going to Europe. There are regular bus services through Eurolines from major European cities, including Ljubljana in Slovenia. If you want to go on a real European adventure, it's entirely possible to leave Sweden (Malmo) on the bus and travel through Denmark, Germany, Switzerland, and then into Italy!

Hiring a car is one of the best ways to take in all the sights of Europe, especially if you have a long journey ahead. In the next chapter, we will cover more about car hire in Italy, but renting a car with a large European company and crossing borders is possible. Be sure to check with the specific companies to ensure that they allow this and that they have a regional office in your final destination. The roads in and around the border areas of Italy are perfect for driving. While you may need to think about winter car equipment during the winter months when passing through the Alps, it can definitely give you a breathtaking journey that you will remember for the rest of your life.

When driving through Europe, be sure to have all the necessary documents. This includes an International Driving Permit and all domestic licenses (paper and card). In addition, of course, you will also need your passport and travel insurance. Most border areas are open and don't usually have long queues, but random checks are being carried out regularly.

Travelling by Ferry

The last option for getting into Italy is via ferry. During the summer, a few ferry services leave Croatia, Greece, Albania, and Montenegro. These will arrive at the southern locations of Venice, Bari, Brindisi, and Ancona. You will also find services that head over to Italy from Corsica (arriving in Genoa) and a ferry from Barcelona that docks in both Genoa and Civitavecchia.

There are several other ferry services worth mentioning, including one that connects Malta and Sicily; another that links Albania with Trieste; and another that connects Italy with Greece. Rates vary depending on the time of year, so it's a good idea to check them out ahead of time before using them. Unfortunately, there are also times when ferry services are canceled due to bad weather in the Mediterranean, especially during the winter months.

Visa Information

Italy is part of the Schengen Zone, which means that people who hold passports from countries that are members of this agreement can visit Italy without having to apply for a visa beforehand. In addition, EU citizens can visit Italy without needing a visa.

Anyone visiting Italy who doesn't hold a passport from an EU or a Schengen country must apply for a Schengen Visa before traveling. This can be done easily, but it will require some paperwork, such as where you intend to stay and proof that you have funds to support yourself for the entire duration of your visit.

You can get the latest information about visas for Italy by checking with your country of origin's embassy or with the Italian consulate in your area. Some countries have different requirements, so getting the correct information on your specific passport is best before your trip.

Chapter 4
Beautiful Rome and Other Notable Places to Visit

Now we're onto the fun stuff!

Indeed, there are many regions in Italy that you can explore, and there are equally as many big cities that you can add to your bucket list! But, it's about streamlining your visit, so knowing where you want to go first and acknowledging that visiting all these places takes time and probably one short vacation won't be enough. But, it gives you a good reason to return to Italy again soon!

Italy's top destinations are filled with amazing sights, meccas of art, cities, and towns full of history and stunning natural landscapes. Here are the best places to visit in Italy:

Roma, Oh Roma!

Of course, whenever you hear the word 'Italy,' you are sure to think of one place – Rome!

First things first - Rome is huge, and Rome is very, very busy! So whether you visit during the summer or winter, there is always a chance to be crowded. However, the heat adds to the experience during July and August, making sightseeing a bit more challenging!

There is so much to see and do in this powerhouse of a city, and that's not just because it is the capital. Rome was the center of the iconic Roman Empire for many years, and you can still see many famous buildings standing today; some may need a little work, but the historical feel is there.

There are several districts within the city itself, but most visitors will stick to the central area, which is relatively small compared with the rest of the city. The center can be divided into two regions - the modern and the old.

The modern central region of Rome is home to big hotels and huge designer shopping outlets, which makes it easy for tourists to shop. However, this area also has pickpockets at work, and you should be careful when walking around this part of the city. If you're into foodie stuff, there are more Italian restaurants here than anywhere else in Rome, but these places tend to cost more due to inflated tourist prices. Make sure not to miss the Trevi Fountain before venturing into the old part of this city, where you'll find many large squares and monuments. The Colosseum is considered the absolute center point of the ancient Roman Empire, so check it out while here!

The Vatican is also part of Rome and a country in its own right. It's always busy and a must on any visitor's list, especially if you're Catholic. You'll find the Vatican Museums here, which house some of the biggest names in art history.

The northern part of the city center is home to the Spanish Steps, a popular tourist destination. The area around Trastevere also has some high-end residential areas and is worth exploring if you're into art. Foodies will find delights at lower prices in Aventino, while nightlife enthusiasts should head to San Lorenzo in the Nomentano area.

Getting around Rome isn't that difficult, but traffic can be horrendous sometimes. Also, driving in Rome can be intimidating. The locals know their way around the city like the back of their hand; therefore, they drive more aggressively or, shall we say, crazily? If you are not used to driving in the middle of a large city, it is best to stick to public transport. Handily there are several modes of transportation you can utilize for your travels in this beautiful city.

There are several public transportation options. One is the Metro service, and the other option is the bus network. Then, of course, there are also taxis but beware of taxi scams—you might be overcharged or not get where you want to go. Most drivers will try to charge you more for the scenic route. It's better to do your research beforehand. This way, you'll know the best route and transportation cost. Don't jump into a cab immediately; try and bargain your price before getting into the car.

Italy's Other Notable Cities and Tourist Spots

Despite Italy's modest size, there is more than enough to see and do. So let's check out the main regions and the wonderful sights you will find within each one. This guide aims to help you plan your visit much more manageable.

Here is a list of Italy's best destinations, a good starting point for having the best holiday here.

The North-West Italy

Northwestern Italy is known for its diversity. The region's capital, Turin, is an elegant city with picturesque palaces, cutting-edge galleries, and delicious dining. While the region might have been one of Italy's 20th-century industrial success stories, it has also retained deep connections to the soil and its wines and culinary offerings, earning it the name of "new Tuscany."

This part of the country is home to the beautiful Italian Riviera, and here you will also find Milan, Genoa, and Lake Como. Moreover, this region is where the Alps are, so you can expect dramatic scenery too! People from all over the world come to this part of Italy to enjoy its spectacular view with French-tinged traditions and to experience skiing or hiking beneath Europe's highest mountains.

ITALIAN RIVIERA (Ligurian Riviera)

- The Italian Riviera is a coastal strip in Italy between the Ligurian Sea and the towering mountains of the Maritime Alps and the Apennines.

- For travelers wanting to enjoy crystal-clear waters and pristine beaches, visiting the famed Italian Riviera cities is a must on your travel itinerary! Bordering the south of the French Riviera (which is home to Monaco), it has been a favorite getaway since the 1800s, not only during the summer but also during off-seasons — mainly because most days are sunny and winters can be mild. Combine that with the Italian Riviera cities' rich histories, picturesque hiking trails, timeless castles, and delectable food, and you have a perfect place for almost any kind of traveler!

- If you want to see more Italian Riviera cities or little towns, then travelling by car is a good choice. It will save you from sorting out train and ferry schedules. However, if you plan to explore places like Cinque Terre or are staying in areas near the coastal train line, it makes more sense to use the public trains.

MILAN

- Milan is Italy's city of the future. It's fast-paced, a place where money talks and creativity is big business. It has an ancient and fascinating history, and after the unification of Italy in 1861, it became an important industrial and cultural center. While it may not have the many historical attractions of other Italian cities, it holds its own with art collections old and new.

- Milan is known for its Duomo Cathedral, La Scala opera house, Sforza Castle and Vittorio Emanuele II shopping arcade. It is also a city that has many cultural landmarks and where fashion, food, and wine culture prevail.

- It will be tough for you to decide what to do first in Milan. But the good news is that you can explore the city in just one day! You'll have time for sightseeing, eating delicious food, shopping, and getting a feel for fast-paced city life.

GENOA

- Genoa is a port city and the capital of northwestern Italy's Liguria region. It has been an important trading center for centuries. As a result, it features many sights related to its maritime past, including the Romanesque Cathedral of San Lorenzo with its distinctive striped facade and frescoed interior. Narrow lanes lead to squares like Piazza de Ferrari, which features an iconic bronze fountain, and Teatro Carlo Felice opera house.

LAKE COMO

- Lake Como, also known as Lake Lario, sits in the shadow of the Rhaetian Alps and is hemmed in on both sides by steep, verdant hillsides. The lake measures around 160km, and its shores are filled with villages, including exquisite Bellagio and Varenna. Where the southern and western shores converge is Como's main town—an elegant, prosperous Italian city.

- Situated in the northern Italian region of Lombardy, Lake Como is known for its luxurious villas and stunning gardens. The mountainous terrain means that opportunities for taking bird's-eye views of the lake and its nearby towns are plentiful. Additionally, with a fraction of the visitors drawn here compared to Lake Garda or Lake Maggiore, Lake Como and its surrounding area offer every traveller a real sense of discovery.

The North-East

Venice and Bologna are two of the largest cities in northeastern Italy, and these are the entry points for most travelers. In addition, Bologna is connected to Florence, Milan, Venice, and Rome by train, and the service at Guglielmo Marconi Airport makes it easy for visitors to fly into another major European city.

In this part of the country, you can expect mountains and hills with some scenic spots to have your photos taken. Parma, Verona, and many ski resorts are here too. Bologna is famous to foodies. Moreover, fans of Romeo and Juliet will undoubtedly want to visit this part of the country for its romantic vibe.

VENICE

-   Venice is a major tourist destination for its celebrated art and architecture. San Marco is probably the most famous and one of the best areas to stay in Venice. When you think of Venice, the image that comes to mind is Saint Mark's Square, or the Bridge of Sighs with a gondola slowly sailing along it. Making your base in San Marco lets you see all the top tourist sights.

-   Piazza San Marco is a popular and crowded public square in Venice, in front of St. Mark's Basilica and Doge's Palace. A small inland waterway separates the square from the palace.

BOLOGNA

-   Bologna is a charming university city home to fine historical buildings and an old medieval center. The place is full of beautiful walkways and squares. It has a rich history, and the cuisine is famous worldwide.

-   This small, picturesque Italian city is worth a visit for anyone who loves authentic Italian food and culture. The medieval UNESCO-listed porticoes of Bologna's old town are illuminated with lights, shadows, and deep architectural perspectives.

The terracotta buildings that span the old town give Bologna its nickname—the "Red City."

PARMA

- If you're looking for a place to visit and see where Parmesan cheese and prosciutto are made—two of Italy's most famous exports—then this small yet prosperous city is worth visiting. There are hardly any cars in the city, so walking or riding a bike will be necessary. This tends to make the visit even more enjoyable.

- If you're looking for something more than just delicious food and a perfect day, Parma is the place to go. Not only will you love the food— Parmigiano Reggiano and prosciutto di Parma (Parma ham) are simply amazing—but you'll also fall in love with the city itself.

VERONA

- Verona is considered one of the most popular travel destinations in Italy for romance because it's between Milan and Venice in northern Italy's Veneto region. The city is famously known as the setting for William Shakespeare's "Romeo and Juliet," but it also has several historical and contemporary attractions.

TRIESTE

- The city of Trieste is famous for its Bora wind. It's a cold, gale-force wind that blows down from the mountains near Mount Triglav, Slovenia.

- Trieste is unique among cities in Europe. It boasts a historic square—Piazza Unità d'Italia—overlooking the sea and a historical landmark fountain, Palazzo del Governo. In addition to exploring the Piazza Unità d'Italia, spend some time exploring Trieste's many other historical sites; check out the Fontana dei Quattro Continenti (fountain), Palazzo del Governo and Trieste Town Hall.

The Heart of Italy

The country's central region is home to the Tuscany area, famed for its rolling hills and wineries. During the summer months, this place is undoubtedly idyllic! You'll also find Abruzzo, Umbria, Rome, and Lazio in this region, as well as Florence, Pisa, and Lucca. As you can imagine, this is one of the most-visited parts of the country due to its famous cities.

TUSCANY

- Tuscany is a central Italy region known for its beauty, history, and influence on the arts. It is home to the birthplace of the Italian Renaissance—and to the many people who are thought to be its most significant artists—and to the language that came from it.

- If you're a UNESCO World Heritage Sites fan, Tuscany is the perfect place to visit. The region is home to seven UNESCO World Heritage Sites, ranging from the prominent (Florence and the Square of Miracles in Pisa) to the relatively obscure (Valdorcia and Pienza).

- Tuscany's best travel months are April, May, June, September, and October. These months offer the convenience of peak season with pleasant weather.

FLORENCE

- Florence is known for its cultural and artistic treasures, including the Uffizi Gallery and the Palazzo Pitti. It is also home to numerous museums and art galleries, such as the Uffizi Gallery and the Palazzo Pitti. These collections continue to influence art, culture, and politics around the world.

- Walking around the city center of Florence can be like stepping back in time. The churches, statues, palazzi, alleys, and markets form a colorful tapestry that blends art and history with modern life's dynamic comings and goings. In June, Florence holds a festival with parades, dances, and games.

PISA

- Pisa is a great place to visit, with many different things to do and see. Of course, the main attraction of Pisa is the Leaning Tower, but there are also many other things worth seeing in this vibrant college town.

- It takes about two hours to see the cathedral without climbing up the Leaning Tower. If you do the tower climb, I'd recommend adding 30 minutes to an hour.

- Tickets to the cathedral are free, but you will need to pick up a ticket and allot a time slot when you arrive or by booking a ticket to another part of the cathedral complex to get a free entry ticket without a time slot.

LUCCA

- Lucca is famous for its music, and each year, there is an annual music festival in Piazza Napoleone hosting artists such as Bob Dylan, John Legend, and the Rolling Stones. However, Lucca is also famous for its opera, so we felt it was only right to attend some Puccini operas in the church he was baptized in.

The South

Amazing weather awaits you in the southern part of the country. It has long been known for its stunning scenery and beautiful towns. This is also where Naples, Capri, Calabria, and the jaw-dropping Amalfi Coast, are located. And, of course, Pompeii, one of the most visited spots of them all.

This region is rich in cultural heritage and is home to some of the most beautiful European cities.

NAPLES

- Naples is the third largest city in Italy, and it's known to be the founding city of pizza. Thanks to its early Greek inhabitants who founded the area centuries ago.

- Located on the western coast of Southern Italy, Naples is one of Italy's major cities' most significant and most productive. It's a huge commercial and public port that accounts for a large percent of the country's economy.

- Naples has many historical sites, including the majestic Castle Nuovo and the San Gennaro Catacombs.

- Moreover, Naples is close to the legendary ruins of both Pompeii and Herculaneum and the epic volcano Mount Vesuvius – these three locations are all must-see attractions when you visit this Italian region.

LECCE

- Lecce is known as the Florence of the South due to its abundance of unique historical structures.

- The city is located in the far south and is famed for its beautiful light Lecce Stone, which has been used to build most of its structures.

- Some of its famous attractions include the beautiful Basilica di Santa Croce, Lecce Castello, and Cattedrale dell'Assunzione della Virgine. Another important site there is the ancient Roman Amphitheatre.

- In Leece, you will also find several remarkable squares, such as the Piazza del Duomo and the Piazza Sant'Oronzo.

- If you don't find historical buildings interesting, you can go to Villa Comunale gardens for some relaxation or check out the excavation of the Faggiano Museum.

THE AMALFI COAST

- The Amalfi coast is one of the most stunning areas in Southern Italy. It stretches from Naples to Salerno and offers dramatic scenery and beautiful towns that embrace the mountains.

- This protected region features idyllic coastal towns that include Amalfi, Erchie, Minori, and Positano. These towns have multi-colored houses stacked against the hillsides and provide picture-perfect photo opportunities.

- Furthermore, the area is filled with opportunities to uncover exciting new sites like the Villa Rufolo in Ravello. The entire region is begging to be explored and to do so you can use a regular train or bus service.

PALERMO

- Palermo is the capital of the island of Sicily and holds an important place in its history. It serves as Sicily's cultural and economic center, where you will find some of the island's most important landmarks. In addition, there are many markets in the city where you can get a good deal with the locals.

- Sicily is an island in the middle of the Mediterranean sea, south of Italy. It's a famous tourist destination and has been heavily influenced by western civilization throughout history.

CAPRI

- Capri is a little island located on the western coast of Southern Italy, near the Amalfi Coast and Naples. The place is gorgeous and well-known as a day trip destination.

- When you get to the island, you'll be amazed at the stunning views of the surrounding area. Then, you can go to Piazzetta and enjoy a drink while enjoying the view. And if you want some adventure, explore the Blue Grotto cave network or take a boat ride around the beautiful island.

Ischia

- Ischia is a volcanic island at the end of the Gulf of Naples. It is much larger than Capri, and both islands are known for their beautiful landscape.

- Here, you will find an active port, a mountain range, and rocky terrain. There are also beautiful villages and marvelous natural gardens.

The Islands

The two main Italian islands are Sicily and Sardinia. These islands offer a picturesque ambiance and a more laid-back way of life. But, of course, you will find remarkable gastronomy on both islands too.

Sicily

- Sicily is famous for its beautiful vineyards, beaches, villages, and cathedrals. You will also find several archaeological sites and ancient ruins.

- It is also known for its world-renowned Sicilian landmarks like The Palermo Opera House and UNESCO Baroque churches in Modica and Noto.

- Sicily is often described as the "magnificent island with multiple souls" because it sums up the Roman, Arab, Hellenic, Byzantine, and Norman splendor.

- Sicily is filled with natural beauty, which makes it an incredibly rewarding destination. Food enthusiasts will also enjoy this place because of its fine cuisine. In addition, the people are warm and friendly.

- If you are wondering if Sicily is expensive to visit – based on European holiday standards, it's pretty affordable. There are Airbnbs, local trattorias, and rental car options that you can use for a holiday that won't break the bank.

Sardinia

- Sardinia is an island paradise that is perfect for a holiday destination. Thanks to its spectacular beaches and exceptional cultural, historical, and natural heritage.

- Sardinia has hot, dry summers and mild winters, which is quite common in many parts of Italy. If you enjoy hot sunny days, the perfect time to visit this place is between June and August.

- Nestled in the Mediterranean, to the west of the mainland. You can move around Sardinia on trains and buses, but if you want to explore the island with free rein, you need to rent a car, motorcycle, or even a bicycle.

How to Get Around Italy

Undeniably, there are so many things to explore in Italy, that's why it's a good thing that there are many ways for you to get around the country. Listed below are some of them:

- **Domestic Flights** - Even though Italy isn't that large compared to other countries, flying between cities might be your best option if you want to save time. This applies if you travel from north to south or vice versa or want to visit the islands. The leading domestic airlines which fly between Italian cities are Alitalia, Meridiana, and Blu-Express. Shop around for tickets and remember that fares will be higher during public holidays and summer.

- **High-Speed Trains** - Italy has a state-of-the-art high-speed train network so that you can travel quickly from one city to another. Some domestic rail networks will accept Eurail passes, e.g., the inter-railing passes we mentioned earlier, but do check as some have specific rules attached to them. If you need to purchase special fares, these aren't usually that high, and if you avoid high peak times and weekends, you can also find good deals. However, a point to remember is to ensure you validate your ticket before getting on the train. You should check whether it has a set date or time on it. You can do this by punching it at the yellow validation boxes at train stations.

- **Buses** - Because the rail network is so which quality, it's far better to use the trains than the buses. For the most part, bus journeys will require trains at some point on the trip anyway. There are many bus stations in most large cities. The long-distance buses run in relatively comfortable surroundings.

- **Boat** - You must travel by boat if you're visiting Venice! Avoid the gondolas if you want to save cash, and instead, take the Vaporetto, a public bus on water and far cheaper. Water taxis are available, but these are pretty expensive. You can also purchase a hop-on and off Vaporetto pass to save cash during your visit. In terms of visiting the islands, you will also see many ferries and hydrofoils which you can use, especially during the summer months.

Driving in Italy

It is entirely doable if you want to rent a car and explore Italy at your own pace. However, as mentioned earlier, driving in Italy can be a daunting experience! In addition, parking can be a huge problem, especially in the main cities; you are likely to spend a lot of time (and cash) trying to find a suitable parking space. This is the reason why most visitors stick to public transport.

Driving in Italy is safe. But, most tourists find it difficult because locals go faster than usual because they are very familiar with the place. It is a common situation that causes fear to most international drivers. There are also many winding streets, especially in cities and large towns. So, if you want a hassle-free and more laid-back experience, you better avoid driving!

But then again, if you are set to go on a road adventure, there are countless international and local car hire companies that you can use. For your convenience, it would be best to stick to those you can find in the main cities or near the airport. You will need an International Driving License and your passport to hire a car. Insurance is also a must-have in Italy, so car hire is a little more expensive, simply because the insurance fee is included in the price. In addition, Italy's fuel cost is relatively higher than other countries.

It's about weighing up your options, but if you're comfortable driving in Italy, you are guaranteed to see far more of the place than doing it otherwise!

Chapter 5
Things to See and Do in Italy

The top destinations you should have on your visit list heavily depend on the area you will be staying in and how much time you have during your trip. There is so much to see and do in Italy that one visit won't be enough unless you stay there for several months. Therefore, you must prioritize a region and plan your trip accordingly to get the most out of it. But at the same time, allow yourself the freedom to wander a bit, too - there are many hidden gems within the country if you take the time to look!

We have discussed in the previous chapter the different regions and the beautiful cities in Italy; this time, we will highlight the main places of interest that you shouldn't miss, especially if visiting Italy for the first time:

- **Explore the City on Water, in Venice** - Venice is one of the world's most beautiful and remarkable cities because it is located on the water! Riding a Vaporetto along the Grand Canal is a true experience. While gondolas might be the more famous option, they'll get you back a considerable amount of Euros! Grab an ice cream (gelato) and take the last Vaporetto ride of the day; it moves slowly, so you will see the incredible sights as you move!

- **Enjoy the Art** - There are many artworks in Italy, and Milan is home to Leonardo da Vinci's 'The Last Supper.' This is so popular that you can only see it for 15 minutes. You'll also need to book your ticket beforehand. If you're a fan of the Renaissance period, then you should head to the Uffizi Gallery in Florence too.

- **Visit the Vatican Museums** – This is one of the must-dos, and if you want to get the most out of it, you should pay for a proper guided tour. By doing so, you will understand and appreciate the place even more. In addition, you can skip the not-so-great stuff and concentrate on the main highlights.

- **Check Out the View From the Florence Duomo** - If you are looking for picturesque sceneries, you would want to check out one of the most jaw-dropping options. But, of course, the best way to do it is by putting your comfortable shoes on and climbing up to the top of the Duomo in Florence. Indeed, there are tight spaces in the area, but the experience is totally worth it!

- **Take a Tour along the Amalfi Coast** – It won't be a good idea to attempt driving along the high cliffs of the Amalfi Coast if you're not the most experienced driver. However, riding a car is the best way to see the natural beauty of Italy at its finest. Many tours are available around the area, so look around for the best deal and grab your camera!

- **Visit The Home of Romeo And Juliet** - Verona is a true cultural delight, and fans of the famous Shakespearean play will surely want to head there! You will find many playhouses in this area, as well as operas that you can check out.

- **Visit 'David' in Florence Galleria dell'Accademia** – This place is a must-do and one that will require queuing! You will also see many notable works of art in this gallery.

- **Explore Pompeii** - If you get the chance to go to Pompeii, take it. This location is like no other - it's a living, breathing, open-air museum! But, of course, Pompeii is a former city that was submerged when Mount Vesuvius erupted in 79AD. So it's an extraordinary sight to see the ruins that this town has today - almost frozen. If you want to discover more, you should head to Naples and the National Archaeological Museum, where many artifacts from Pompeii are on display.

- **Go hiking on the Cinque Terre** - This vast hiking trail is extremely popular and crowded during summer. Despite that, it is a great way to see the natural area and some of the most authentic villages. It shouldn't take more than a day at the very most if you take your time.

- **Visit Rome's Pantheon** - The Pantheon is free, which means many tourists visit this place. Despite that, it's a wonderfully historic place to visit, being over 2000 years old!

- **Explore Tuscany During The Summer** - There is something truly idyllic about Tuscany at any time of the year, but the entire scenery seems to come to life during the summer months. Whether you're a wine fan or not, the landscapes are always a delight. This will certainly fill up your camera's memory card. So enjoy the place and take as many pictures as you can!

- **Go to The Colosseum** - When you visit Rome, you must go to the site of ancient gladiator battles and the very place where Julius Caesar once stood. You will find that it is indeed a historical place with plenty of people lining up!

- **Climb Mount Etna** - Yes, you can climb an active volcano! Head to Sicily and visit the mighty Etna.

There are many walking tours around that the locals are arranging. This way, you can discover the place safely and enjoy the mesmerizing views with a guide to show you the beautiful spots.

- **Stand in Awe at The Sistine Chapel** - You probably have seen pictures of it, but nothing will prepare you for seeing it in person. Michelangelo's masterpiece is truly amazing and one you shouldn't miss.

- **Go to The Opera in Milan** - La Scala is one of the world's most famous opera houses, and it's still functioning to this day. So if you want a night with the rich and famous, go and watch a performance. But be sure to purchase tickets well ahead of time because the tickets run out fast.

- **Enjoy Skiing in the Alps** - The Italian Alps are breathtaking, and during the winter months, you can enjoy skiing in many distinguished resorts. Livigno is a good spot for total beginners, while Val Gardena is an excellent choice for more advanced skiers.

- **Chill Out in Capri, Sardinia, or Sicily** - If you want to escape the mainland and enjoy the island way of life, hop on a ferry and head over to one of the islands for a quiet time. Remember that Sicily will always be busy during the summer, but there are hidden coves you can explore; just ask some locals where they usually go!

- **Photo Op at The Leaning Tower of Pisa** – Almost everyone who has been to Pisa has taken that iconic photo. Remember, it's not going to fall over. It just looks like it might! And if you want to explore the place, you can climb to the top of the tower for more amazing views and photos!

- **Marvel at Lake Como's Scenery** - Lake Como is a breathtakingly beautiful place. That is why you should have it on your list. Many wealthy and famous celebrities have also visited this place and acquired some properties.

- **Explore the Vatican City** – It is home to the most iconic sights, including the Basilica of St. Peter and St. Peter's Square. You can't simply visit Italy and not head to the most famous part – especially if you are a catholic!

- **Explore the Roman Forum** - While in Rome, make sure you visit the Roman Forum. This place will give you a glimpse of their life during the Roman Empire. The buildings and the ruins will surely amaze you.

- **Milan's Famous Duomo** - Officially known as the Cathedral of Santa Maria Nascente, this is one of the world's largest churches and a truly amazing sight to behold. If you are a fan of architecture, you will be captivated by the Gothic style and the intricate details of this place. But, of course, you can also go to the top floor by using an elevator and have a look over Milan. But, then again, you can expect crowds in this place.

- **Head to Ponte Vecchio, Florence** - The Old Bridge is one of the most beautiful sights in Florence. A lot of history is connected to the bridge, which relates back to WWII. It's a perfect place to take lots of photographs!

- **Make a Wish at The Trevi Fountain** – This is another of Rome's top destinations. If you throw a coin over your shoulder into the fountain, legend says you will return to the city. If you throw two coins, you will fall in love with a gorgeous Italian. And if you throw three coins, you will marry the person you fell in love with. The money thrown into the fountain is estimated to be around 3000 Euros daily and given to chosen charity.

- **The Amazing Blue Grotto of Capri** – When you visit Capri, visit the Blue Grotto. This is a sea cave on the coast of the island. The water glows a stunning shade of blue when the sun cascades inside. It is one of those attractions that even photographs cannot do justice with. To go to this place, you need to ride a rowboat and duck because the entrance to the cave is relatively low, just one meter in height!

- **Go skiing and hiking in the Dolomites** - You can practice skiing in the Dolomites in the winter and go hiking in the summer. The landscapes are breathtaking, and you can visit Marmolada, the highest mountain, at 3343 meters high.

- **Go shopping in Milan** - If you want to indulge in retail therapy, you'll find lots of places to do that all over Italy, but one city, in particular, is iconic - Milan! It is one of the world's most fashionable cities, and here you can check out the big designer names and might end up doing some expensive shopping along the way.

Italy is a land of beauty and adventure. It offers so much to those who take the time to explore its many treasures. With warm locals who will happily guide you to anything about the place, you are visiting and perhaps even tell you a legend or famous story along the way. Surely, you will enjoy every minute of your time in this wonderful country.

We do recommend that you spend some time discovering more about the country. These places offer the most beautiful, historical, and cultural experiences. So plan your time wisely and make sure that you explore the areas thoroughly before attempting to tick them off your list!

However, there is one thing we have yet to discuss thoroughly, which most visitors enjoy more than anything else in Italy – the food!

Let's find out more in the next chapter!

Chapter 6
Food, More Food, and Coffee!

Italy is famous for many things, and the food is one of them!

Pizza, pasta, gelato, and coffee are some of the world's most famous foods, and they all came from Italy!

It's no wonder that many people visit this wonderful country for its renowned gastronomy. And if you want to learn how to make them the Italian way, you can join a pasta workshop or a pizza class while you are there!

You probably have been to an Italian restaurant, perhaps in your hometown, but nothing can prepare you for the most authentic Mediterranean dishes Italy offers. Of course, Naples is the home of the famous pizza, and if you're a pizza lover, better add its birthplace to your itinerary! But, of course, no matter where you are heading in Italy, the food is delightful.

There aren't words good enough to describe their food!

So, if you're unsure where to start your Italian gastronomic adventure, let's check out some of the must-tries (if you haven't already!)

- **Pizza** - We've just mentioned previously that pizza was born in Naples, but you'll find it in various places all over the country. The most famous pizza variety is Napoletana. But, there are many other options, making it challenging to narrow down a favorite! You will notice that the authentic Italian pizza isn't made in a deep pan. Instead, it's a thin, crispy crust cooked in a wood fire oven. But, if you want to try the most authentic pizza, you should go for Napoletana, which consists of fresh and juicy tomatoes, mozzarella, and olive oil. Simple yet extremely delicious because they use the finest ingredients!

- **Lasagna** - It is one of the most famous types of pasta. Lasagna is a favorite dish in Italy! Popular in Bologna, lasagna is cooked pasta sheets baked with beef, cheese sauce, tomato sauce, and lots of herbs. It is usually served with more cheese on top. It is also Garfield's favorite food, and who can blame him? There are a few variations, but you'd better stick to the classic for the natural flavors!

- **Ossobuco Alla Milanese** As the name suggests, this dish comes from Milan, and it is a juicy cut of veal cooked in broth with white wine and vegetables. Sumptuous and very filling dish!

- **Panzanella** - This is a type of salad you will find mainly in Tuscany. This dish is filling because it has bread, tomatoes, onions, and cucumber. It is often served with a tangy olive oil vinaigrette.

- **Focaccia** – This bread is so famous not only in Italy but elsewhere in the world. You might have heard or eaten this in the past. Focaccia is an Italian bread that originated in the city of Genoa, and you can also find them in many other parts of the country. The bread is usually brushed with olive oil and sprinkled with aromatic herbs like rosemary or basil for a more delightful flavor.

- **Spaghetti Alla Carbonara** - This pasta dish that many people love originated in Rome. It consists of spaghetti, eggs, cheese, pork or bacon, and black pepper - so creamy and delicious! In many other countries, you will find that cream is added to the recipe. However, that is not the traditional way of cooking it.

- **Polenta** – This Italian dish is traditionally prepared with cornmeal, ground rice, buckwheat flour, and Parmesan cheese. It can be made in many ways, but the porridge-like side dish is the most popular. This is usually served alongside Osso Buco, short ribs, and stewed oxtail. It also makes a perfect base for vegetables such as baked mushrooms or roasted broccoli.

- **Risotto** – It may look like typical rice, but it isn't. It is a popular Italian dish made with special high-starch, short-grain rice such as Italian Arborio, Vialone Nano, or Carnaroli rice. This kind of rice can absorb more liquid than the regular ones. The traditional risotto recipe is cooked with butter, Parmesan cheese, and fresh herbs. Although this dish has many variations, the most popular ones in Italy are those with seafood, fish, chicken, and vegetables.

- **Gelato** – This is a favorite Italian dessert. This take on classic ice cream has spread across the country. You can find kiosks or shops that offer various flavors!

- **Tiramisu** - One of the tastiest desserts you can try and widely popular in Italy is Tiramisu. A cake-like dessert made with layers of homemade whipped cream, an egg yolk-enriched mascarpone filling, and coffee-soaked ladyfingers.

The next thing that we will talk about is another favorite among locals and tourists in Italy - Yes, Coffee!

In Italy, coffee is a way of life. You can find locals enjoying sitting outside a local cafe, sipping a cup of coffee and watching the world go by. This is also a way of bringing people together and chatting about everything from politics to the weather. Caffè (coffee) is the Italian word for coffee, but it also refers to what they order at a coffee shop; the most common type of espresso.

There are particular recommendations for the Italian way of drinking coffee like the following:

- Drink milky coffee drinks in the morning
- Drink stronger coffee drinks after midday and espresso to finish the day
- The three main types of breakfast coffee are a cappuccino, café latte, and latte macchiato

The cappuccino is one of the most popular types of coffee in Italy. It consists of espresso, steamed milk, and milk foam—all mixed together in equal parts. Italians drink cappuccinos only in the morning because it's rich in milk; other than that time, they prefer tea or Caffè lungo.

However, it is not done to order cappuccinos after noon. Some say it's because the milk and foam make for a nutritious replacement for a meal, and dairy upsets the digestion.

Coffee in Italy is a little stronger than you might be used to, so that is certainly something to bear in mind! Italians also finish an evening meal with a coffee, but this is a strong version, such as an espresso.

Chapter 7
Save Cash, Do More in Italy

After reading our last two chapters about things to see and do and the foods to eat, you're probably preparing your finances and planning your trip as quickly as possible. That's a great idea! Italy is a European country, meaning that prices aren't the cheapest but not the most expensive.

Looking around the place, you can find great deals. It is best to shop and dine where most locals go. You can also find accommodations with meals that are more budget-friendly. If you want to save, you should avoid public holidays and weekends. It's about being smart and checking the rates beforehand to catch the best deals.

Of course, this is a country which you would want to get the most out of. So, here are some tips on how to save cash and do more when in Italy.

Plan Your Dates Carefully

We have already discussed in the previous chapter that certain public holidays and celebrations occur annually in Italy. If you can avoid these times, you will likely save cash on flights and accommodation, and it will be less stressful for you to travel around. In addition, you should avoid the peak season (July to August) because prices are costly during the summer months. The off-season and the shoulder seasons are the perfect times to visit, not only because of lower accommodation rates but also because of fewer tourists or crowds. The weather isn't terrible during the winter, but if you prefer the fair weather more, check out spring and autumn rates for a moderate climate choice.

Search Around For Flights

If you fly long distances, look for indirect flights to save cash. Spending a few hours for a layover in another country is really not that bad. Alternatively, you can monitor the rates of different airlines and book when they are at their lowest. Many airlines have flash sales or seat sales, and by checking regularly, you can save some money which you can use for other travel expenses.

Look at Staying in Hostels

The big cities (Rome especially) have plenty of hostels which are far cheaper than most hotels. On the other hand, some of the large hotel chains can be very expensive, especially during the summer months. But, if you are going to be out sightseeing most of the time, why do you need a costly hotel room? Many hostels are of high quality and centrally located, saving you time and cash.

Ask the Locals Where They Eat

Since Italian cuisine is very popular, most restaurants in the big cities usually charge very high prices, even for regular dishes. In this case, ask a hotel staff or waiter in a cafe where they usually go for their evening meal. If you can go where the locals go, you'll get more authentic dishes for much lesser price.

Look out for Free Activities to Save Cash

Yes! There are free activities in Italy, such as the Pantheon in Rome! Try to include as many of these activities as possible in your itinerary. Then, save money for other popular attractions you want to see. You could also check out walking tours to see a lot in a short time.

Check the Exchange Rates Regularly

Italy's currency is Euros, which has favorable rates in most cases. Therefore, if you watch the exchange rate before you travel and change your money once you arrive, you will likely get more Euros for your cash and have more money to spend.

Avoid Gondolas

This has been mentioned previously, but it's a money-saving tip to consider. While you might have seen romantic gondola rides on TV, they are expensive and not as romantic as they look! On the other hand, water taxis (Vaporettas) are just as much fun and far cheaper.

Be Careful With Taxis

The long-time scam or trick of taking visitors around the city on a more extended trip than necessary is widespread in Italy, especially in Rome. So make sure you either don't use taxis or make it very clear to the driver that you know where you're going and how much the journey should cost. Most drivers will insist on the meter, but do your research about the costs ahead of time to avoid unnecessary overspending.

Avoid Buying Water When Visiting Restaurants

Water in restaurants is costly, and while you might not think much of it, it will all add up in the long run! Buy one or two refillable bottles and simply fill them up whenever you can for constant supply; this way, you will stay hydrated (which is vital, especially in the summer months) and save cash too.

Pre-book Train Tickets

Italy's rail network is undoubtedly a quick and efficient way to get around the country. But you will save cash if you pre-book your tickets ahead of time. Use rail passes wherever possible, and avoid turning up on the day. Otherwise, you pay a higher price, and over time those extra Euros would add up, and you will waste significant amounts.

Walk Wherever Possible

Italy's big cities are all walkable; if you do so, you will discover many hidden gems! So put some comfortable shoes on and start exploring soon as you arrive in the city. This way, you will save cash on taxis or other public transport services while enjoying many beautiful views.

Stand up in Cafes, Don't Sit Down

Our final money-saving tip is one you might not have thought of - stand up when visiting a cafe. Yes, because if you sit down, you may find that your coffee costs more. When you go into a cafe, ask if they charge more for seating, and if they do, stand up or just order a takeaway. So you can start roaming around while enjoying a cup of coffee!

Remember that every money you save would mean you have more to spend elsewhere!

Conclusion

Now you're ready to pack your suitcase and book a flight to Italy! This book should help you learn many things about this amazing country. It is highly recommended that you highlight the main points that have been discussed in this book so you can quickly go back to them when the need arises.

Indeed, this beautiful country has a lot to offer, especially for first-time travellers. However, it has more tourist destinations than most other countries, so you must plan your time carefully to ensure you get the most out of your visit.

Know the purpose of your travel, it could be about sightseeing, shopping, nature, and beach experience, or you simply want to learn more about their history and culture. Whatever it is, you should be able to identify your travel goals and prioritize the things you like most.

Pick the best travel dates for you. If you don't like too much crowd and heat, then avoid July to early September. During these months, the heat is up, and most attractions are full of tourists, especially in Rome. If you avoid these months, you will likely get better deals and get to visit less crowded places during your stay.

Indulge and try out their local food and coffee because nothing compares to what they have in Italy. They use the finest and freshest ingredients to prepare food and beverages; that is why many people love Italian cuisine.

Finally, take lots of photos of every destination you visit, so you can capture the beauty of the place and all the happy moments you've had during your trip.

Printed in Great Britain
by Amazon